CELEBRATE UGLY!

Jessie Oleson Moore

T0364016

RP Minis®
Hachette Book Group
1290 Avenue of the Americas, New York, NY 10104
www.runningpress.com
@Running_Press

First Edition: September 2024

Published by RP Minis, an imprint of Hachette Book Group, Inc. The RP Minis name and logo is a registered trademark of Hachette Book Group, Inc.

Running Press books may be purchased in bulk for business, educational, or promotional use. For more information, please contact your local bookseller or the Hachette Book Group Special Markets Department at Special.Markets@hbgusa.com.

The publisher is not responsible for websites (or their content) that are not owned by the publisher.

Design by Justine Kelley

ISBN: 978-0-7624-8470-6

CONTENTS

INTRODUCTION

When the weather outside is frightful,
there's nothing more delightful than
donning your ugliest Christmas sweater.
From festive reindeer pullovers to
vintage snowflake knits to over-the-top
toppers jam-packed with holiday designs
and doodads, ugly Christmas sweaters

are a beloved holiday tradition—and they're as ubiquitous as they are hideous. You probably have one in your closet. *Maybe you're wearing one right now.*

Here's a shocker: Unsightly holiday sweaters haven't always been à la mode. Until quite recently, they were even mocked. So, how on earth did they go from a dorky way to deck yourself out to Santa-approved sartorial sensations?

It's nothing short of a Christmas miracle. In this book, you'll learn what your preferred sweater says about you and—the real reason you're here—how to throw the ultimate ugly Christmas sweater party.

What Your Ugly Christmas Sweater Says About You

What kind of message does your ugly Christmas sweater of choice say about you? Let's find out . . .

ULTRA-IRONIC HOLIDAY SWEATER

WHAT IT IS: This sweater isn't merely ugly—it's absurd. Think Santa riding a T-rex or a unicorn. Better yet, Santa battling a dinosaur while riding a unicorn.

WHAT IT SAYS ABOUT YOU: Sure, you're willing to play this ugly sweater game, but you want to make it clear that you're doing it with a sense of irony. Advice? Drink some eggnog, chill out, and surrender to the joy of the season, sans the snarkiness.

FAVORITE CHRISTMAS SONG: "Christmas Wrapping"

VINTAGE
CHRISTMAS SWEATER

WHAT IT IS: A vintage sweater featuring busy rows of homey holiday motifs; it may be two-color or multicolored. This is the closest you'll get to the original Jingle Bell sweaters.

WHAT IT SAYS ABOUT YOU: You're a sucker for tradition. Hallmark holiday movies legit make you a little teary-eyed. You love wrapping gifts ornately and your holiday card list is massive. You own multiple sets of holiday pajamas.

FAVORITE CHRISTMAS SONG:

"Winter Wonderland"

TRICKED-OUT CHRISTMAS TREE SWEATER

WHAT IT IS: The concept behind this merry maximalist sweater is quite simple: Take all the Christmas trimmings like tinsel, ornaments, and lights, and instead of your tree, stick them on yourself.

WHAT IT SAYS ABOUT YOU: You *lurve* Christmas. If you could exist in an endless holiday montage, you would. So why not dress the part? Your sweater may be visual overload but that's the way you like it.

FAVORITE CHRISTMAS SONG: "Rockin' Around the Christmas Tree"

HAPPY
REINDEER FACE
SWEATER

WHAT IT IS: Rudolph is front and center on this iconic holiday print that features a reindeer face, often with embellishments or add-ons.

WHAT IT SAYS ABOUT YOU: You're not conflicted about the commercialization of the season. In fact, you might even say it makes you glow. You love giving and receiving holiday gifts, and you totally organized—and baked cookies for—the white elephant gift exchange at work.

FAVORITE CHRISTMAS SONG: "Rudolph the Red-Nosed Reindeer" (Obvi.)

**CAT
UGLY CHRISTMAS
SWEATER**

WHAT IT IS: Just what it sounds like: A Christmas sweater with a cat front and center. Frequently, it will include a feline pun like "Merry Meowmas," "Santa Claws," or "Whisker Wonderland."

WHAT IT SAYS ABOUT YOU: You're a cat person—duh. You probably got your cat(s) Christmas presents (yes, plural)—possibly a holiday outfit, too. Simply put, you love your cat and this is the *purrfect* ugly Christmas sweater for you.

FAVORITE CHRISTMAS SONG: The entire *Jingle Cats* album

BIG GOLD BOW CHRISTMAS SWEATER

WHAT IT IS: Santa baby, where's the mistletoe? This flirty sweater features a gigantic gold bow that makes you look like a big, wrapped present.

WHAT IT SAYS ABOUT YOU: Your presence is the present! You're the life of the party and always in demand under the mistletoe. But you're just as nice as you are naughty and always bring a thoughtful host gift to every holiday party.

FAVORITE CHRISTMAS SONG: "All I Want for Christmas Is You"

UGLY
CHRISTMAS SWEATER
VEST TWINSET

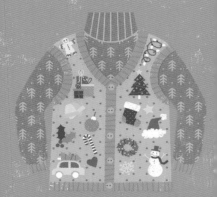

WHAT IT IS: A one-two punch of ugly: A Christmas-themed turtleneck topped with a sweater vest adorned with holiday embellishments.

WHAT IT SAYS ABOUT YOU: You honestly don't know this sweater is ugly—you think it's both fun and functional. Your favorite typeface is probably comic sans. But that's okay because you're probably a kindergarten teacher. (Or a kindergartner.)

FAVORITE CHRISTMAS SONG: "Jingle Bells"

WHAT IT IS: A sweater with a smiling snowman often surrounded by holiday icons like candy canes or snowflakes.

WHAT IT SAYS ABOUT YOU: You're sincerely kind and enthusiastic about everything, including the holidays. You're not the center of attention, but you're a great holiday party guest. You socialize with everyone, are happy to make a beer run, and you probably even brought party games.

FAVORITE CHRISTMAS SONG: "Frosty the Snowman"

GNOME
HOLIDAY SWEATER

WHAT IT IS: A milder version of the ultra-ironic Christmas sweater—a little tongue-in-cheek but worn in a convivial spirit. This type of sweater frequently includes a pun like "I'll Be Gnome for Christmas."

WHAT IT SAYS ABOUT YOU: You like your holidays with a dose of good humor. If someone needs to dress up as Santa or an elf, you're quick to volunteer. You always choose punny holiday cards because they just *sleigh* you!

FAVORITE CHRISTMAS SONG: "Wonderful Christmastime"

FLASHY GINGERBREAD MEN CHRISTMAS SWEATER

WHAT IT IS: A jazzy little number with gregarious gingerbread people often featuring a busy background with holiday icons and designs. Don't stare at it too long—you might get dizzy.

WHAT IT SAYS ABOUT YOU: This sweater commands attention, which is a good thing, because you want to cover up the fact that you wore your comfy pants. Happily, with a bright and bold focal point like this, you can be festive *and* cozy.

FAVORITE CHRISTMAS SONG: "It's Beginning to Look a Lot Like Christmas"

How To Throw the Best Ever Ugly Christmas Sweater Party

GIVE A LITTLE BIT: The first ugly Christmas sweater party was a fund-raiser—and a successful one at that. Why not follow suit? 'Tis better to give than receive, so consider asking for charitable contributions to donate to those in need.

BRING ON THE CHRISTMAS SPIRITS: There's no faster or more effective way to get people feeling holly-jolly than giving them a little booze—eggnog or spiced mulled wine are always a good idea. Be sure to have some non-alcoholic potables on hand, too—hot apple cider, hot choco-late, etc.

DON'T FORGET FOOD: It can get ugly in unanticipated ways if you give people drinks and no food. Remember: Kitsch is the name of the game at an ugly Christmas sweater party. Here's your

 chance to whip up a Jell-O mold or some pigs in a blanket!

DECK THE WALLS: Embrace the tacki-ness of the theme and load up on all the tinsel, garish lights, and decorations you can. Be creative! Garden gnomes with Christmas lights? Garland of retro troll dolls with holiday-hued hair? *Chef's kiss*

MERRY MUSIC: A holiday playlist is a must! Be sure to add all the favorite Christmas songs from this book, as well as other holiday hits.

PARTY ACTIVITIES: Don't just leave people standing around looking ugly. Here are a few jolly and joyful activities to consider: ugly Christmas sweater pageant; gingerbread man decorating; DIY ornament stations.

PARTY FAVORS, BABY! Need a few festive ideas? Mini stockings filled with candy; tiny sweater wine cozies; copies of this mini kit . . .